PRENTICE HALL MATHEMATICS

ALGEBRA 1

Reading and Math Literacy Masters

PEARSON

Prentice Hall

Needham, Massachusetts
Upper Saddle River, New Jersey

ISBN: 0-13-068620-4

10   06

Contents

A Spanish version of the Reading and Math Literacy Masters is available.

To the Teacher

To solve problems and become math literate students must be able to extract important information from words and symbols. The activities in these masters help students analyze written material and math symbols and build their math vocabularies in order to become better problem solvers and better test-takers.

Study Skill Tips

Each master begins with a brief Study Skill tip to help students improve their studying skills and their test-taking skills.

Reading and Math Literacy Activities

Each chapter has four activities to help students as they work through the chapter.

Chapter Organizer

The **Chapter Organizer** activity should be used at the beginning of each chapter. The top part of the master is a chapter-survey activity; the bottom part is a graphic organizer. Have students complete the chapter survey when the Chapter Opener is introduced. Students can then fill in the graphic organizer as they work through the chapter. The completed graphic organizer is a particularly valuable study tool for reviewing the chapter material.

Reading/Writing Math Symbols

The **Reading/Writing Math Symbols** activities are positioned for use at either Checkpoint Quiz 1 (Master B) or for use at Checkpoint Quiz 2 (Master C). These masters include activities such as giving verbal and pictorial meaning to a symbol, matching symbols with words/definitions, using symbols as shorthand, or deciphering symbols within diagrams (e.g., right angle marker).

Reading Comprehension

The **Reading Comprehension** activities are positioned for use with either Checkpoint Quiz 1 (Master B) or for use with Checkpoint Quiz 2 (Master C). These masters include activities such as sequencing, following directions, reading math sentences, using logic, or translating words into math.

Vocabulary

Use the **Vocabulary** activity at the end of each chapter. The vocabulary used in the activity may be cumulative within the particular course. For example, Chapter 7 may include key terms from Chapters 1–6. Vocabulary masters include activities such as crossword puzzles, scrambles, fill-in-the-blanks, matches, and any activity that makes use of math terms.

1A: Graphic Organizer

For use before Lesson 1-1

Study Skill: Always write down your assignments. Do not rely on your memory to recall all assignments from all your classes.

Write your answers.

1. What is the chapter title? _____

2. Find the Table of Contents page for this chapter at the front of the book. Name four topics you will study in this chapter.

    _____   _____

    _____   _____

3. What is the topic of the Reading Math page? _____

4. What is the topic of the Test-Taking Strategy page? _____

5. Look through the pages of the chapter. List four real-world connections that you see discussed in this chapter.

    _____   _____

    _____   _____

6. Complete the graphic organizer below as you work through the chapter.
    *   In the center, write the title of the chapter.
    *   When you begin a lesson, write the lesson name in a rectangle.
    *   When you complete a lesson, write a skill or key concept in an oval linked to that lesson block.
    *   When you complete the chapter, use this graphic organizer to help you review.

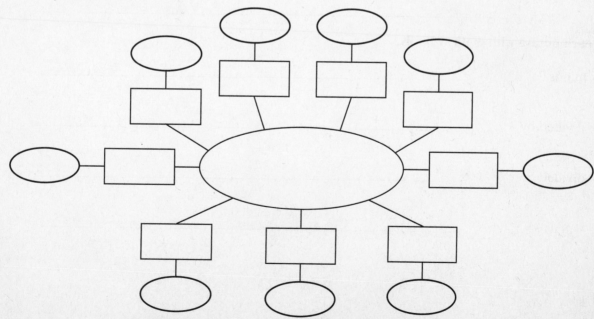

1B: Reading/Writing Math Symbols

For use after Lesson 1-4

Study Skill: When you take notes in class, keep up with what is being said if you use abbreviations. Use abbreviations that you will be able to understand when you review your notes.

Mathematics is a language made up of symbols that represent words and amounts. For example, the mathematical expression 5 × 2 symbolizes five times two.

Explain the meaning of each mathematical expression using words.

1. $3 \cdot 7$ _____

_____

2. $5n$ _____

_____

3. $3 \div 4$ _____

_____

4. $\frac{7}{12}$ _____

_____

5. 2^x _____

_____

6. $6(7)$ _____

_____

Write each phrase with math symbols.

7. 7 minus 3 _____

8. p divided by 2 _____

9. 4 divided by x _____

10. y equals 9 _____

1C: Reading Comprehension

For use after Lesson 1-8

Study Skill: When you read a paragraph, it is a good idea to read it twice: once to get an overview, then again to find the essential information.

Read the passage below and answer the following questions.

> The blue whale is the largest animal on earth. A blue whale is about 100 million times larger than the krill, one of the smallest creatures it eats. The skeleton of a blue whale can weigh about 50,000 pounds. The heart of a blue whale can be the size of a small car. The largest recorded blue whale weighed 160 tons. About how much of that weight was *not* the skeleton?

1. What is the subject of this paragraph? _____

2. What are the numbers 50,000 and 160 in the paragraph referring to?

   _____

3. What question are you asked to answer? _____

   _____

4. What is the weight (and the units) for the skeleton? _____

5. Which is the smaller unit of measure, pounds or tons? _____

6. What is the total weight of the largest blue whale? _____

7. What units are used for the total weight of the largest blue whale? _____

8. How can you change 160 tons into pounds? _____

   _____

9. Write an equation to find how much of the whale's weight is *not* the skeleton.

   _____

10. Solve the equation to answer the question asked in the paragraph.

    _____

1D: Vocabulary

For use with Chapter Review

Study Skill: Many words in English have more than one meaning. Often a word has one meaning in ordinary conversation, and a different specific meaning or exact definition when it is used in math or science or grammar. You can often figure out which meaning to use by looking at the sentence that contains the word. To help you decide what a word means, consider the surroundings, or context, in which you see the word.

Read the mathematical definition in the left column and the sentence in the right column. In the blank in the middle, write the one word from the list below that fits both the definition and the sentence. The first one is done for you.

base	like	origin	constant
natural	power	element	open
real	term		

Definition   **Sentence**

1. kind of number in a set of rational and irrational numbers together   _____real_____   It is a _____ event. It actually happened.

2. a term that has no variable   _____   That noise is _____. It just never seems to stop.

3. a number that is multiplied repeatedly   _____   Put this statue on its _____ so it will not fall over.

4. the kind of terms that have exactly the same variable factors   _____   I really _____ that kind of food. It is my favorite.

5. the kind of math sentence that has one or more variables   _____   The door should be _____ so the customers can come in.

6. the base and exponent of an expression of the form a^n _____   Turn off the _____ before you try to repair those wires.

7. the kind of number you might use to count rocks or pencils   _____   Let's go for a walk by the lake. I want to enjoy the _____ world.

8. the point where the axes of a coordinate plane intersect   _____   What is the _____ of that custom? I wonder how it began.

9. a number, a variable, or the product of a number and one or more variables   _____   He will come home from college at the end of the _____.

10. the name of each item in a matrix   _____   One _____ in water is oxygen. The other is hydrogen.

2A: Graphic Organizer

For use before Lesson 2-1

Study Skill: Keep notes as you work through each chapter to help you organize your thinking and to make it easier to review the material when you complete the chapter.

Write your answers.

1. What is the chapter title? _____

2. Find the Table of Contents page for this chapter at the front of the book. Name four topics you will study in this chapter.

    _____   _____

    _____   _____

3. What is the topic of the Reading Math page? _____

4. What is the topic of the Test-Taking Strategy page? _____

5. Look through the pages of the chapter. List four real-world connections that you see discussed in this chapter.

    _____   _____

    _____   _____

6. Complete the graphic organizer below as you work through the chapter.
    - In the center, write the title of the chapter.
    - When you begin a lesson, write the lesson name in a rectangle.
    - When you complete a lesson, write a skill or key concept in an oval linked to that lesson block.
    - When you complete the chapter, use this graphic organizer to help you review.

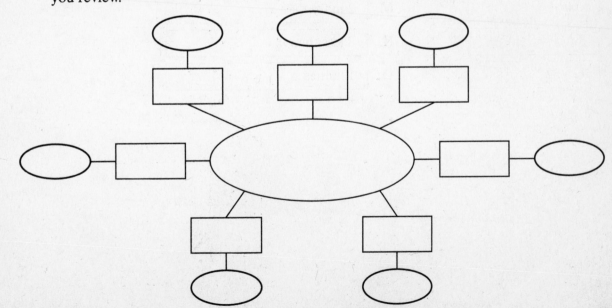

2B: Reading/Writing Math Symbols

For use after Lesson 2-3

Study Skill: When you take notes in any subject, it helps if you learn to use abbreviations and symbols such as @ (at); #, #s (number, numbers); w/ (with); w/o (without); s/b (should be).

Match the symbolic expression in Column A with its written expression in Column B by drawing a line between them.

	Column A			Column B
1.	$2 + x$		**A.**	quotient of r and 32
2.	$\frac{r}{3}$		**B.**	absolute value of negative 6
3.	$-12 \div x$		**C.**	18 decreased by r
4.	$18 - r$		**D.**	14 subtracted from k
5.	$\frac{1}{3}x$		**E.**	the sum of x and y
6.	$\lvert -6 \rvert$		**F.**	100 minus w
7.	$x + y$		**G.**	negative 12 divided by x
8.	$h - 8$		**H.**	one-third of x
9.	$12 + y$		**I.**	twice w
10.	$12x$		**J.**	12 greater than y
11.	$2w$		**K.**	exceeds x by 32
12.	$k - 14$		**L.**	r divided into 3 parts
13.	$100 - w$		**M.**	2 more than x
14.	$\frac{r}{32}$		**N.**	8 less than h
15.	$x + 32$		**O.**	12 times x

2C: Reading Comprehension

Study Skill: Some mathematics problems require a large amount of reading. It is important to be able to separate relevant from non-relevant information. Analyze word problem(s) carefully, read thoroughly, and then ask yourself questions to clarify what was asked.

Read the paragraph below and follow what Andrea thinks and writes.

> Louis and Robin are returning to college after their winter break. They are each returning to a different college. The colleges are located 650 miles apart in opposite directions. They plan to leave their parents' home at 8:00 A.M. Both leave at the same time and travel on a straight road in opposite directions. Robin drives 12 mi/h faster than Louis. After 4 hours, they are 472 miles apart. Find Louis's and Robin's speed.

What Andrea Thinks	What She Writes
I'll read the problem and write down the important information.	Robin drives 12 mi/h faster than Louis. 4 hours = 472 miles apart
Where should I start? It always helps to find formulas that pertain to the given information and to write sentences based on that information.	rate $\times$ time = distance The distance Robin travels + the distance Louis travels = 472 miles.
Now, I'll define some variables. The problem asks for each person's speed and relates Robin's speed to Louis' speed.	Let x = Louis' speed. Let $x + 12$ = Robin's speed.
Now I can write an equation and solve it.	rate $\times$ time = distance Louis' distance + Robin's distance = total distance. $4x + 4(x + 12) = 472$ $4x + 4x + 48 = 472$ $8x = 424$ $x = 53$ $x + 12 = 65$
Now, I need to go back and make sure that I answer the question asked.	Louis was driving 53 mi/h and Robin was driving (53 + 12) or 65 mi/h.

Place a check beside each statement that is not relevant to solving the problem.

____ speeds Robin and Louis were traveling   ____ the time they were traveling

____ the distance between the colleges   ____ travel in opposite directions

____ They both planned to leave at 8:00.   ____ returning to college after break

____ Robin has a heavy foot.   ____ They both left at the same time.

2D: Vocabulary

For use with Chapter Review

Study Skill: When you complete a puzzle such as a word search, remember to read the list of words carefully and completely. As you identify each word in the word search, circle it and then cross off the word from the list. Pay special attention to the spelling of each word.

Complete the word search.

base	coefficient	coordinates
equation	exponent	identity
inequality	integers	matrix
mean	median	mode
opposite	origin	outlier
power	quadrants	range
reciprocal	simplify	variable

```
C  S  W  Z  X  D  I  F  Y  K  A  L  R  M  P
T  N  E  I  C  I  F  F  E  O  C  A  P  A  Z
L  I  J  T  E  M  I  G  E  D  Y  C  U  T  N
S  E  D  D  A  L  E  Q  N  T  T  O  N  R  A
D  R  O  E  P  N  U  D  I  W  L  R  O  I  E
R  M  E  M  N  A  I  L  I  C  Y  P  U  X  M
T  E  I  G  T  T  A  D  B  A  E  I  T  J  A
N  S  W  I  E  U  I  M  R  D  N  C  L  W  T
E  B  O  O  Q  T  N  T  L  O  T  E  I  U  F
N  N  H  E  P  Z  N  C  Y  N  O  R  E  O  T
O  P  N  E  L  B  A  I  R  A  V  C  R  O  S
P  I  Q  U  A  D  R  A  N  T  S  I  R  L  N
X  O  P  P  O  S  I  T  E  E  G  N  A  R  M
E  S  U  B  A  S  E  J  M  I  D  C  S  T  U
G  C  N  G  W  P  C  G  N  Z  H  L  L  X  C
```

3A: Graphic Organizer

Study Skill: Before you start your new chapter, read the major headings and summaries. This will give you a good idea of what the entire chapter will be about.

Write your answers.

1. What is the chapter title? _____

2. Find the Table of Contents page for this chapter at the front of the book. Name four topics you will study in this chapter.

   _____   _____

   _____   _____

3. What is the topic of the Reading Math page? _____

4. What is the topic of the Test-Taking Strategy page? _____

5. Look through the pages of the chapter. List four real-world connections that you see discussed in this chapter.

   _____   _____

   _____   _____

6. Complete the graphic organizer below as you work through the chapter.
   - In the center, write the title of the chapter.
   - When you begin a lesson, write the lesson name in a rectangle.
   - When you complete a lesson, write a skill or key concept in an oval linked to that lesson block.
   - When you complete the chapter, use this graphic organizer to help you review.

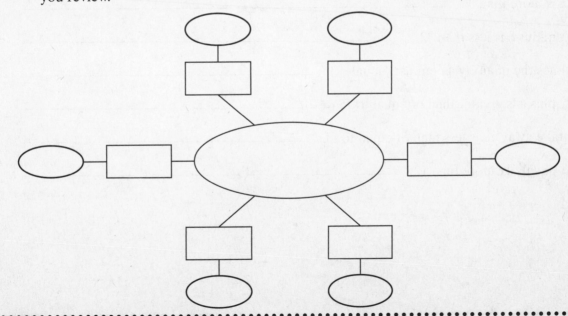

3B: Reading/Writing Math Symbols

For use after Lesson 3-3

Study Skill: Keep your homework in a special notebook or section in a loose-leaf binder. This way you will always be able to find it quickly.

Write how to read each symbol.

1. < _____

2. > _____

3. ≤ _____

4. ≥ _____

5. = _____

Write how to read each expression.

6. $8 > 4$ _____

7. $12 < 25$ _____

8. $3x \leq 15$ _____

9. $4x + 2 \geq 12$ _____

10. $12x = 36$ _____

Write each phrase in symbols.

11. 8 is less than 12 _____

12. 17 is greater than 2 _____

13. $12x$ is more than 36 _____

14. $15x$ minus 8 is less than 32 _____

15. 8 times the quantity $4x$ minus 3 equals 21 _____

16. $10x$ plus 4 is greater than or equal to 15 _____

17. $3x$ take away 12 is less than or equal to 21 _____

18. $32x$ equals $4x$ more than 12 _____

3C: Reading Comprehension

For use after Lesson 3-5

Study Skill: It is a good idea to read the question at the end of a word problem first so that you know what you are looking for when you read the rest of the problem.

When reading a word problem, it is sometimes difficult to determine which inequality sign should be used. Match each expression in Column A with the correct inequality symbol or expression in Column B by drawing a line between them. Some answers may be used more than once. Some may not be used at all.

Column A		Column B	
1.	is less than	**A.**	$\geq$
2.	is greater than	**B.**	$c > j$
3.	is less than or equal to	**C.**	$<$
4.	is greater than or equal to	**D.**	$c < j$
5.	is at most	**E.**	$m \geq b$
6.	is at least	**F.**	$l \geq w$
7.	l is no more than w	**G.**	$m < b$
8.	m is no less than b	**H.**	$>$
9.	Connie (c) is not as tall as Jose (j).	**I.**	$l > w$
10.	Cory (c) is older than Janishia (j).	**J.**	$\leq$
11.	Luana (l) is at least as tall as Whin (w).	**K.**	$m \leq b$
12.	Marty (m) is at most the same height as Brie (b).	**L.**	$l \leq w$

Name_____ Class_____ Date_____

3D: Vocabulary

For use with Chapter Review

Study Skill: You will encounter many new terms as you read a mathematics textbook. Read aloud or recite the new terms as you read them. This will help you remember and recall rules, definitions and formulas for future use. It is important to learn the definitions of new terms as soon as they are introduced and continue to increase your vocabulary.

Unscramble the UPPERCASE letters to form a math word or phrase that completes each sentence. Copy the letters in the numbered cells to the cells with the same number at the bottom of the page.

1. COOPDUNM EUNIISAQELTI are joined by *and* or *or*.
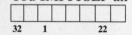
   6   16   13

2. An TEITINYD is an equation that is true for every value.
   19 20 3

3. The NRGEA of a set of data is the difference between the greatest and least data values.
   5

4. A data value that is much higher or lower than the other data in a set is an LEUTORI.
   9

5. An XENNPTEO shows repeated multiplication.
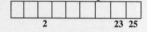
   28   15 14

6. A coordinate plane is divided by its axes into four TANQAUSRD.
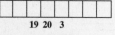
   2   23 25

7. You IMPIYSLF an equation when you replace it with its simplest name or form.
   32 1   22

8. A EVBALRAI is a symbol, usually a letter, which represents one or more numbers.
   12   18

9. The numerical factor when a term has a variable is a CINCEFFITOE.
   26 21 31   10 27 24 29 8

10. LOHWE SURBEMN are the nonnegative integers.
    4   17   11

11. The multiplicative inverse of a number is always its RLREIPACCO.
    30   7

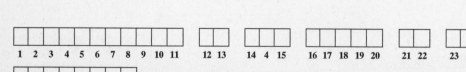
 1 2 3 4 5 6 7 8 9 10 11   12 13   14 4 15   16 17 18 19 20   21 22   23 4 24

 25 26 27 28 29 30 31 32

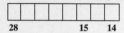
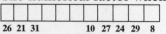
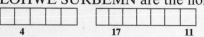
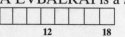

4A: Graphic Organizer

For use before Lesson 4-1

Study Skill: As you read over the material in the chapter, keep a paper and pencil handy to write down notes and questions that you have. You should read ahead of the teacher. It will help you understand some of the material better.

Write your answers.

1. What is the chapter title? _____

2. Find the Table of Contents page for this chapter at the front of the book. Name four topics you will study in this chapter.

    _____   _____

    _____   _____

3. What is the topic of the Reading Math page? _____

4. What is the topic of the Test-Taking Strategy page? _____

5. Look through the pages of the chapter. List four real-world connections that you see discussed in this chapter.

    _____   _____

    _____   _____

6. Complete the graphic organizer below as you work through the chapter.
    • In the center, write the title of the chapter.
    • When you begin a lesson, write the lesson name in a rectangle.
    • When you complete a lesson, write a skill or key concept in an oval linked to that lesson block.
    • When you complete the chapter, use this graphic organizer to help you review.

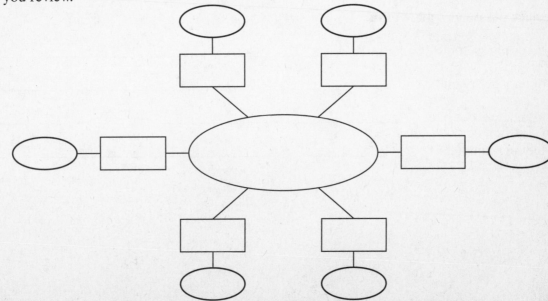

4B: Reading/Writing Math Symbols

For use after Lesson 4-2

Study Skill: There are many symbols that are abbreviations for longer words. Using these symbols when taking notes helps you keep up with the person giving the notes. Learn these symbols for quicker note-taking.

Write what each abbreviated math symbol means.

1. ¢/oz _____

2. mi/h _____

3. ft/min _____

4. km/h _____

5. ft/mi _____

6. $/yr _____

7. $/lb _____

8. ft/wk _____

9. gal/wk _____

10. mi/gal _____

11. lb/in.^{2} _____

12. ft/sec.^{2} _____

13. m/sec.^{2} _____

14. $/oz _____

Write each phrase in symbol form.

15. miles per gallon _____

16. dollars per pound _____

17. kilometers per hour _____

18. feet per minute _____

Name _____ Class _____ Date _____

4C: Reading Comprehension

Study Skill: When solving percent problems be sure to read each problem carefully. Look for the word *is*. If the two numbers that are given to you are on the same side of *is*, then the numbers are multiplied.

Read each problem and determine if the equation that follows it is correct. If it is, write "correct." If it is not, correct it. The first two are done for you.

Problem	Equation	Written Correctly
1. What percent of 125 is 75?	$125x = 75$	correct
2. 10 is 5% of what number?	$10 \times 0.05 = x$	$10 = 0.05x$
3. How much is 30% of 150?	$x = 0.30 \times 150$	
4. 25% of 180 is what number?	$0.25 \times 180 = x$	
5. 27.5% of 152 is what number?	$\frac{152}{27.5} = x$	
6. What percent of 48 is 24?	$\frac{48}{24} = x$	
7. What percent of 82.5 is 132?	$\frac{82.5}{132} = x$	
8. 20% of what number is 45?	$0.20x = 45$	
9. $\frac{3}{4}$% of what number is 11.25?	$0.0075x = 11.25$	
10. Specifications for bronze call for 80% copper. How much copper is needed to make 200 lb of bronze?	$0.80 \times 200 = x$	
11. Because of wear, a 90-hp engine is operating at 75% of its horsepower. How much horsepower is 75% of the 90-hp engine?	$\frac{90}{0.75} = x$	
12. A newspaper ad offered a set of tires at a sale price of $275. The regular price was $300. What percent of the regular price were the savings?	$\frac{275}{300} = x$	
13. A DVD with a regular price of $18 is on sale this week at 20% off. Find the amount of the discount.	$0.18(20) = x$	
14. Marcus makes 6% commission on every house he sells. What is his commission on an $80,000 sale?	$\frac{80,000}{0.06} = x$	

4D: Vocabulary

For use with Chapter Review

Study Skill: One of the most difficult things about reading a mathematics textbook is the new vocabulary you will encounter. Often you encounter several new terms in each section. Mathematics is a series of concepts you need to learn and remember. It is important to learn the definitions of new terms as soon as they are introduced. Read aloud or recite the new terms as you read them. Reciting a rule, definition or formula can help you to remember and recall it.

Match each term in Column A with its definition in Column B by drawing a line between them.

Column A	Column B
1. event	A. the data item or items that occur(s) the greatest number of times in a set
2. percent of increase	B. the difference between the greatest and least data values
3. compound inequality	C. the four sections on a coordinate plane
4. outcome	D. a numerical factor of a term with a variable
5. probability	E. a term that has no variable
6. quadrants	F. two inequalities that are joined by the word "and" or the word "or"
7. ratio	G. a comparison of two numbers by division
8. mode	H. how likely it is that something will occur
9. constant	I. a reduced or enlarged drawing that is similar to an actual object or place
10. scale drawing	J. the percent of change when an amount increases
11. proportion	K. a rate with a denominator of 1
12. coefficient	L. any outcome or group of outcomes
13. percent of decrease	M. the result of a single trial
14. range	N. the percent of change when an amount decreases
15. unit rate	O. an equation stating that two ratios are equal

5A: Graphic Organizer

For use before Lesson 5-1

Study Skill: Develop and use a standard method of note-taking, including punctuation and abbreviations. Take and keep your notes in a large notebook. A large notebook will allow you to adequately take notes and jot down information without running out of paper or space.

Write your answers.

1. What is the chapter title? _____

2. Find the Table of Contents page for this chapter at the front of the book. Name four topics you will study in this chapter.

   _____   _____

   _____   _____

3. What is the topic of the Reading Math page? _____

4. What is the topic of the Test-Taking Strategy page? _____

5. Look through the pages of the chapter. List four real-world connections that you see discussed in this chapter.

   _____   _____

   _____   _____

6. Complete the graphic organizer below as you work through the chapter.
   • In the center, write the title of the chapter.
   • When you begin a lesson, write the lesson name in a rectangle.
   • When you complete a lesson, write a skill or key concept in an oval linked to that lesson block.
   • When you complete the chapter, use this graphic organizer to help you review.

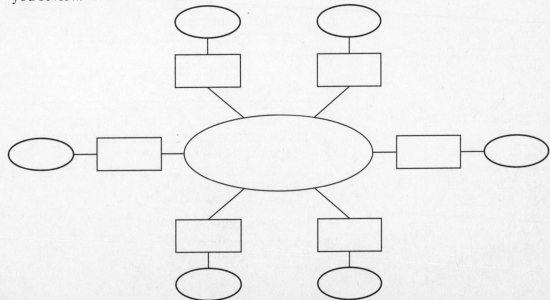

5B: Reading/Writing Math Symbols

For use after Lesson 5-2

Study Skill: When you take notes in any subject, it helps if you learn to use abbreviations and symbols that represent words. You should also use math symbols whenever possible.

Match the symbolic expression in Column A with its written expression in Column B by drawing a line between them.

	Column A		Column B
1.	$k - 14 < 12$	**A.**	miles per gallon
2.	$12 + y$	**B.**	dollars per pound
3.	$\lvert -4 \rvert$	**C.**	15 times x equals 12 more than x
4.	$15x = 12 + x$	**D.**	twelve times x
5.	ft/wk	**E.**	12 is greater than or equal to twelve times x
6.	km/h	**F.**	w divided into 4 parts
7.	\$/gal	**G.**	kilometers per hour
8.	$12x$	**H.**	a number take away 14 is less than 12
9.	$21 - w$	**I.**	twelve plus y
10.	$12 \geq 12x$	**J.**	21 decreased by w
11.	$\frac{w}{4}$	**K.**	dollars per gallon
12.	25%	**L.**	absolute value of the quantity x plus 4 is greater than or equal to 5
13.	$12 < x$		
14.	\$/lb	**M.**	twenty-five percent
15.	mi/gal	**N.**	seventeen less than w
16.	$\lvert x + 4 \rvert \geq 5$	**O.**	feet per week
17.	$\frac{1}{4}x$	**P.**	5 times a number x is less than or equal to 25
18.	$5x \leq 25$	**Q.**	12 is less than a number x
19.	$w - 17$	**R.**	4 divided into w parts
20.	$4 \div w$	**S.**	absolute value of negative four
		T.	one-fourth of x

5C: Reading Comprehension

Study Skill: After reading a section, try and recall the information. Ask yourself questions about the section. If you cannot recall enough information re-read portions you had trouble remembering. The more time you spend studying a paragraph, the more you can recall.

Read the problem and follow along with Carlita as she solves the problem.

> The weight of an object on Earth is directly proportional to the weight of the same object on the moon. A 220-lb astronaut would weigh 36 lb on the moon. How much would a 40-lb dog weigh on the moon?

What Carlita Thinks	What Carlita Writes
I will read the problem and write down the important information.	220 lb astronaut = 36 lb on moon 40 lb dog = ?
Where should I start? It says the object is directly proportional, so I will set up a proportion.	$\dfrac{\text{astronaut weight on Earth}}{\text{astronaut weight on moon}} = \dfrac{\text{dog weight on Earth}}{\text{dog weight on moon}}$
Since I am looking for the dog weight on the moon, I will let that be x. I will now substitute the information I am given into the proportions.	$\dfrac{\text{astronaut weight on Earth}}{\text{astronaut weight on moon}} = \dfrac{\text{dog weight on Earth}}{\text{dog weight on moon}}$ $\dfrac{220}{36} = \dfrac{40}{x}$
Now I can solve the proportion.	$\dfrac{220}{36} = \dfrac{40}{x}$ $220x = 1440$ $\dfrac{220x}{220} = \dfrac{1440}{220}$ $x = 6.54$
I'll write my answer in a sentence.	The weight of the dog on the moon is approximately 6.5 lb.

Read the following problems and solve.

1. The volume of a can of corn is proportional to the height of the can. If the volume of the can is 300 cm³ when the height is 10.62 cm, find the volume of a can with a height 15.92 cm.

2. The number of servings of meat that can be obtained from a turkey varies directly as it weight. From a turkey weighing 16 kg, one can get 42 servings of meat. How many servings can be obtained from a 10-kg turkey?

5D: Vocabulary

For use with Chapter Review

Study Skill: When you read, your eyes make small stops along a line of words. Good readers make fewer stops when they read. The more stops you make when you read, the harder it is for you to comprehend what you've read. Try to concentrate and free yourself of distractions as you read.

Complete the crossword puzzle.

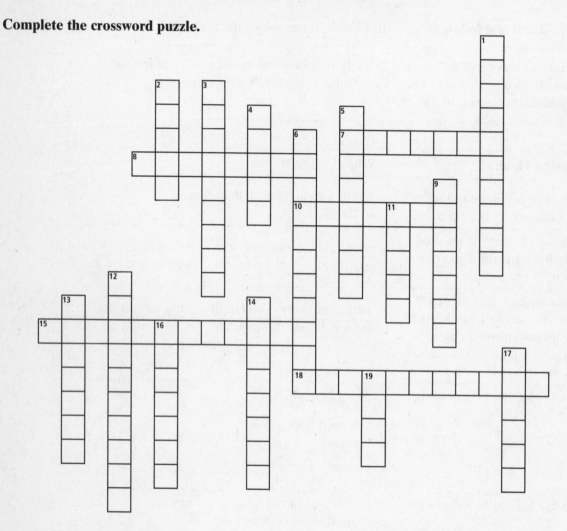

ACROSS	4. set of second coordinates in an ordered pair
7. the result of a single trial	5. a term that has no variable
8. a number pattern	6. rational numbers and irrational numbers
10. an equation involving two or more variables	9. each item in a matrix
15. an equation that describes a function	11. a comparison of two numbers by division
18. a graph that relates two groups of data	12. multiplicative inverse
	13. a data value that is much higher or lower than any other data values in the set
DOWN	14. a relation that assigns exactly one value in the range to each value in the domain
1. a conclusion you reach by inductive reasoning	16. operations that undo each other
2. has two parts, a base and an exponent	17. the set of first coordinates in an ordered pair
3. type of reasoning where conclusions are based on patterns you observe	19. each number in a sequence

6A: Graphic Organizer

For use before Lesson 6-1

Study Skill: When taking notes do not try and write down everything that the teacher is saying. It is impossible to do. Spend more time listening and write down the main points and examples. If you are writing as fast as you can, you cannot be listening as well.

Write your answers.

1. What is the chapter title? _____

2. Find the Table of Contents page for this chapter at the front of the book. Name four topics you will study in this chapter.

   _____   _____

   _____   _____

3. What is the topic of the Reading Math page? _____

4. What is the topic of the Test-Taking Strategy page? _____

5. Look through the pages of the chapter. List four real-world connections that you see discussed in this chapter.

   _____   _____

   _____   _____

6. Complete the graphic organizer below as you work through the chapter.
   • In the center, write the title of the chapter.
   • When you begin a lesson, write the lesson name in a rectangle.
   • When you complete a lesson, write a skill or key concept in an oval linked to that lesson block.
   • When you complete the chapter, use this graphic organizer to help you review.

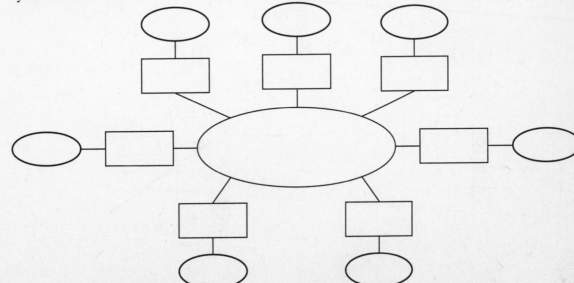

6B: Reading Comprehension

For use after Lesson 6-3

Study Skill: Reading and interpreting diagrams, graphs, and charts is an important skill in algebra and in everyday life. Whether you are studying for an algebra test or reading the newspaper, the text is often accompanied by a graph or diagram. When you read diagrams, graphs, and charts, pay close attention to the details they contain.

Determine whether each graph below represents a function or a relation. If the graph represents a linear function, give the slope and *y*-intercept.

1.
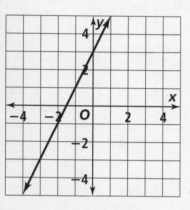

2.
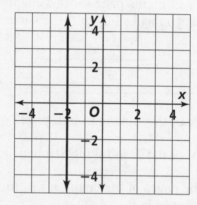

3.
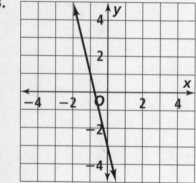

4.
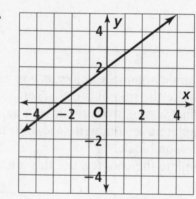

5.
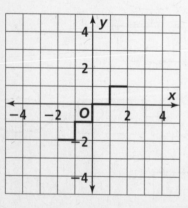

6.
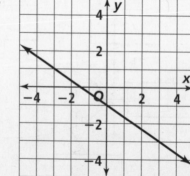

Reading and Math Literacy Masters

Algebra 1

6C: Reading/Writing Math Symbols

For use after Lesson 6-6

Study Skill: Many times you need to refer to concepts taught in previous lessons. Use the Table of Contents or Index to quickly locate these concepts.

Write what each of the symbols, variables, or equations represents. The first one is done for you.

1. $(x, 0)$ _____ x-intercept _____

2. $>$ _____

3. $|x|$ _____

4. $\perp$ _____

5. $\geq$ _____

6. $y = mx + b$ _____

7. $<$ _____

8. $Ax + By = C$ _____

9. $=$ _____

10. $\|$ _____

11. m, in $y = mx + b$ _____

12. b, in $y = mx + b$ _____

13. $\leq$ _____

14. $-x$ _____

15. $(0, y)$ _____

16. $\times$ _____

6D: Vocabulary

Study Skill: Always read direction lines before doing any exercises. What you think you are supposed to do may be quite different than what the directions call for.

Circle the word that best completes the sentence.

1. (*Parallel lines, Perpendicular lines*) are lines in the same plane that never intersect.

2. The point where a line crosses the *y*-axis is known as the (*x-intercept, y-intercept*).

3. The linear equation $y = mx + b$ is in (*slope-intercept, point-slope*) form.

4. The (*slope, equation*) of a line is its rate of vertical change over horizontal change.

5. Two lines are (*parallel, perpendicular*) if the product of their slopes is -1.

6. A (*slope, translation*) shifts a graph horizontally, vertically, or both.

7. The (*domain, range*) of a relation is the set of second coordinates in the ordered pairs.

8. An equation that describes a function is known as a (*function rule, function notation*).

9. (*Dependent, Independent*) events are events that do not influence one another.

10. The (*mean, median*) is the middle value in a set of numbers when arranged in numerical order.

11. A power has two parts, a (*base, coefficient*) and an exponent.

12. A(n) (*exponent, variable*) is a symbol, usually a letter, that represents one or more numbers.

13. The (*absolute value, reciprocal*) of a number is its multiplicative inverse.

14. The equation $3 + 4 = 4 + 3$ illustrates the (*Identity Property of Addition, Commutative Property of Addition*).

15. When a value is less than its original amount, the percent of (*increase, decrease*) can be found.

16. The (*complement of an event, experimental probability*) consists of all the outcomes not in the event.

17. A V-shaped graph that points upwards or downwards is the graph of a(n) (*linear, absolute value*) equation.

18. Another name for a number pattern is a (*conjecture, sequence*).

7A: Graphic Organizer

For use before Lesson 7-1

Study Skill: When taking notes make your original notes as easy to read as possible. Use abbreviations of your own invention when possible. The amount of time needed to recopy messy notes would be better spent rereading and thinking about them.

Write your answers.

1. What is the chapter title? _____

2. Find the Table of Contents page for this chapter at the front of the book. Name four topics you will study in this chapter.

   _____   _____

   _____   _____

3. What is the topic of the Reading Math page? _____

4. What is the topic of the Test-Taking Strategy page? _____

5. Look through the pages of the chapter. List four real-world connections that you see discussed in this chapter.

   _____   _____

   _____   _____

6. Complete the graphic organizer below as you work through the chapter.
   • In the center, write the title of the chapter.
   • When you begin a lesson, write the lesson name in a rectangle.
   • When you complete a lesson, write a skill or key concept in an oval linked to that lesson block.
   • When you complete the chapter, use this graphic organizer to help you review.

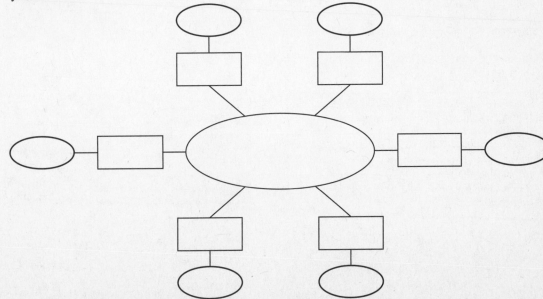

7B: Reading/Writing Math Symbols

For use after Lesson 7-2

Study Skill: Review notes that you have taken in class as soon as possible to clarify any points you don't clearly understand and to refresh your memory.

Many graphs look extremely similar. You must look for details in the graphs and their equations, and determine what those details symbolize. Look at each inequality, and then choose its correct graph.

1. $y \geq 3$

A. 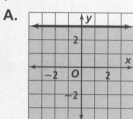 B. 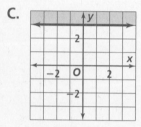 C. 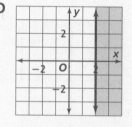 D.

2. $x < 2$

A. 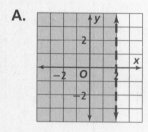 B. 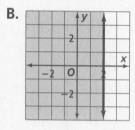 C. 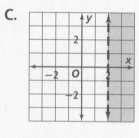 D.

3. $y \leq x + 2$

A. 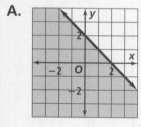 B. 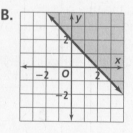 C. 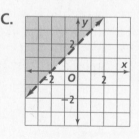 D.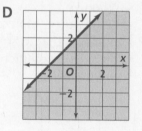

4. $y > 2x + 5$

A. 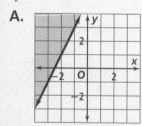 B. 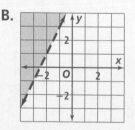 C. 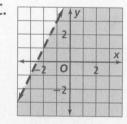 D.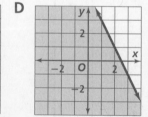

7C: Reading Comprehension

For use after Lesson 7-5

Study Skill: Reading a mathematics textbook requires being able to extract important information from a graph, figure, diagram, or picture. Take time to look over diagrams carefully, looking for relationships between lines, points, etc.

Follow the thought process that Matthew thinks and writes.

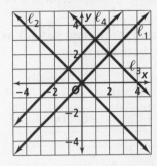

In the graph, a quadrilateral is formed by four intersecting lines denoted ℓ_1, ℓ_2, ℓ_3, and ℓ_4. Find the equation of each line and determine the best description of the quadrilateral.

What Matthew Thinks	What Matthew Writes
I have to find the equations of four lines. What information appears to be true about the lines?	There appears to be two pairs of parallel lines. If that is true, there will only be two slopes. The shape also appears to be a rectangle. If that is true, the two slopes will be negative reciprocals of each other since the lines are perpendicular.
What do I know about ℓ_1? I must look at the diagram to find points that the line passes through.	ℓ_1 passes through $(0, 0)$ and $(2, 2)$. $m = \frac{2 - 0}{2 - 0} = 1$ The y-intercept is 0. The equation of ℓ_1 is $y = x$.
What do I know about ℓ_2? I will use points from the diagram again.	ℓ_2 passes through $(0, 0)$ and $(-1, 1)$. $m = \frac{1 - 0}{-1 - 0} = -1$ The y-intercept is 0. The equation is $y = -x$.
What do I know about ℓ_3? By looking at the diagram, I think that this is the line that is parallel to ℓ_2.	ℓ_3 passes through $(2, 2)$ and $(0, 4)$. $m = \frac{4 - 2}{0 - 2} = \frac{2}{-2} = -1$ The y-intercept is 4. The equation is $y = -x + 4$. The slopes of ℓ_2 and ℓ_3 are the same so they are parallel.
What do I know about ℓ_4? By looking at the diagram, I think that this is the line that is parallel to ℓ_1.	ℓ_4 passes through $(0, 2)$ and $(-2, 0)$. $m = \frac{0 - 2}{-2 - 0} = \frac{-2}{-2} = 1$ The y-intercept is 2. The equation is $y = x + 2$. The slopes of ℓ_1 and ℓ_4 are the same so they are parallel.
What is the best description of the quadrilateral?	Opposite sides are parallel and the two slopes are negative reciprocals, so the quadrilateral is a rectangle.

Exercises

1. Three vertices of a rectangle are at $(1, 1), (5, 1)$ and $(5, 5)$. Find the equation of each line forming the rectangle.

2. One side of a square has vertices at $(2, 3)$ and $(-2, 1)$. What is the slope of the adjacent sides?

7D: Vocabulary

For use with Chapter Review

Study Skill: To be successful in mathematics you need to be able to understand meanings of words that you know and ones that you don't. Learn each term one at a time, moving on to the next when you are confident of your knowledge of the first.

Match each term in Column A with its definition in Column B by drawing a line between them.

Column A		Column B	
1.	system of linear equations	A.	a comparison of two numbers by division
2.	element	B.	two or more linear equations using the same variables
3.	solutions of an inequality	C.	any ordered pair that makes all of the equations in the system true
4.	constant	D.	a term that has no variable
5.	linear inequality	E.	multiplicative inverse
6.	parallel lines	F.	lines in the same plane that never intersect
7.	elimination method	G.	a method of solving systems of equations by replacing one variable with an equivalent expression
8.	variable	H.	a number pattern
9.	ratio	I.	each item in a matrix
10.	outcome	J.	a method of solving a system of equations by adding or subtracting equations to eliminate a variable
11.	substitution method		
12.	conjecture	K.	has 2 parts, a base and an exponent
13.	power	L.	the rate of vertical change to horizontal change of a line
14.	solution of the system	M.	a region of the coordinate plane that has a boundary line
15.	sequence	N.	a symbol that represents one or more numbers
16.	system of linear inequalities	O.	the coordinates of the points that make the inequality true
17.	reciprocal	P.	a conclusion reached by inductive reasoning
18.	slope	Q.	two or more linear equalities taken together
		R.	the result of a single trial

Name _____ Class _____ Date _____

8A: Graphic Organizer

Study Skill: When taking notes, write down everything written on the chalkboard or overhead. What you write down may be a clue as to what might be on an exam or test.

Write your answers.

1. What is the chapter title? _____

2. Find the Table of Contents page for this chapter at the front of the book. Name four topics you will study in this chapter.

   _____   _____

   _____   _____

3. What is the topic of the Reading Math page? _____

4. What is the topic of the Test-Taking Strategy page? _____

5. Look through the pages of the chapter. List four real-world connections that you see discussed in this chapter.

   _____   _____

   _____   _____

6. Complete the graphic organizer below as you work through the chapter.
   - In the center, write the title of the chapter.
   - When you begin a lesson, write the lesson name in a rectangle.
   - When you complete a lesson, write a skill or key concept in an oval linked to that lesson block.
   - When you complete the chapter, use this graphic organizer to help you review.

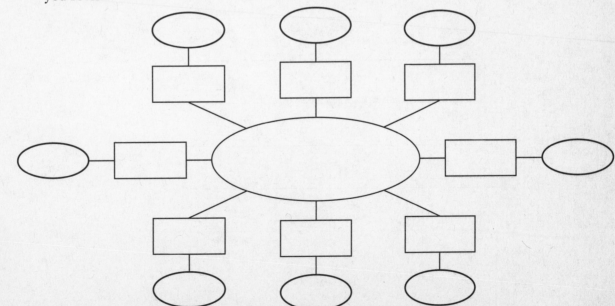

Algebra 1

8B: Reading/Writing Math Symbols

For use after Lesson 8-4

Study Skill: After completing your homework, take a break. Then come back and check your homework. You will sometimes discover mistakes that you could not see when you were in the process of doing your work.

Write how you would read each of the following expressions. The first one has been done for you.

Expression   **Read as:**

1. $2x^3y^4$ _____2 times x cubed, y to the fourth power_____

2. 4^{-3} _____

3. x^2 _____

4. (xy) _____

5. $(x^2)^3$ _____

6. $(y^3z^4)^2$ _____

7. $\dfrac{x}{y}$ _____

8. $\left(\dfrac{y^2}{x^4}\right)^5$ _____

9. $5x \cdot y^4$ _____

10. $x^5 + x^5$ _____

11. $\sqrt{x^2y}$ _____

12. $8x^2 - 3y$ _____

13. $\dfrac{8y^3}{3x^8}$ _____

14. $\dfrac{x^2}{x^8}$ _____

15. $4x^{11}$ _____

8C: Reading Comprehension

Study Skill: You often need to follow written directions. Read them carefully and slowly, and do not skip any steps.

The following procedure can be used to measure the height of tall objects.

Step 1. Draw a vertical line to represent the tall object.

Step 2. Draw a horizontal line to represent the object's shadow.

Step 3. Draw a vertical line to represent the height of something you can measure, such as your height or the height of a mailbox.

Step 4. Draw a horizontal line to represent the shadow of the measurable object.

Step 5. Connect endpoints of the segments to make two similar triangles.

Step 6. Measure the second object and the two shadows, and label each corresponding part of the drawing. Make sure the measurements are in the same unit. Label the missing height x.

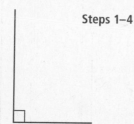 Steps 1–4   Steps 5 and 6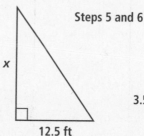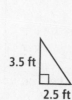

Step 7 Write a proportion.

$$\frac{\text{tall object's height}}{\text{tall object's shadow}} = \frac{\text{measurable object's height}}{\text{measurable object's shadow}} \Rightarrow \frac{x}{12.5} = \frac{3.5}{2.5}$$

Step 8 Solve the proportion.

$2.5x = 43.75$ Write cross products.

$\ x = 17.5$ The unknown height is 17.5 feet.

Use the steps above to find the missing heights.

1. Mark needs to determine the height of a radio tower. He measured the shadow of the tower and found that it was 40 ft long. His own shadow was 3 ft long. If Mark is 6 ft tall, how tall is the radio tower?

2. Celia needed to find the height of a tree for her botany report. She measured the shadow of the tree and found it was 5 m long. Her own shadow was 0.8 m long. If Celia is 1.6 m tall, how tall is the tree?

3. A girl who is 172 cm tall wants to find the height of a flagpole. If her shadow is 120 cm and the shadow of the flagpole is 4.5 m, how tall is the flagpole? (*Hint:* Make sure all units are the same before calculating.)

8D: Vocabulary

Study Skill: Always read direction lines before doing any exercises. What you think you are supposed to do with an activity may be quite different than what the directions call for.

Circle the word that best completes the sentence.

1. A number in (*standard form, scientific notation*) is written as a product of two factors in the form $a \times 10^n$, where n is an integer and $1 \le a < 10$.

2. Each number in a sequence is called a (*term, constant*).

3. In a(n) (*arithmetic, geometric*) sequence you multiply a term in the sequence by a fixed number.

4. The (*Substitution, Elimination*) method is a way of solving systems of equations by replacing one variable with an equivalent expression.

5. A system of linear equations has (*no solution, many solutions*) when the graphs of the equations are parallel lines.

6. In the function $f(x) = 5^x$, as the values of the domain increase, the values of the range (*increase, decrease*).

7. When a bank pays interest on both the principal and interest the account has already earned, the bank is paying (*simple, compound*) interest.

8. A(n) (*interest, growth*) period is the length of time over which interest is calculated.

9. In a relation the first set of coordinates in the ordered pairs is called the (*domain, range*).

10. A base and an exponent are the two parts of a (*symbol, power*).

11. Lines in the same plane that intersect to form a 90° angle are said to be (*perpendicular, parallel*).

12. The (*median, mode*) of a collection of data is the data item that occurs most often.

13. The result of a single trial is called the (*outcome, probability*).

14. Each item in a matrix is called a(n) (*term, element*).

15. In the exponential function $y = a \cdot b^x$, $a > 0$ and $b > 1$, the base (b) is the (*decay, growth*) factor.

16. $-2, 4, \frac{1}{2}, \frac{3}{4}, -8, 6$ are examples of (*real numbers, integers*).

9A: Graphic Organizer
For use before Lesson 9-1

Study Skill: To remember the math concepts, you can study with a friend.
Quiz each other on the details of the algebra rules and procedures. Use
your notes to help you determine possible test questions. Reviewing right
before bedtime will help you retain the material you study.

Write your answers.

1. What is the chapter title? _____

2. Find the Table of Contents page for this chapter at the front of the book.
   Name four topics you will study in this chapter.

   _____   _____

   _____   _____

3. What is the topic of the Reading Math page? _____

4. What is the topic of the Test-Taking Strategy page? _____

5. Look through the pages of the chapter. List four real-world connections
   that you see discussed in this chapter.

   _____   _____

   _____   _____

6. Complete the graphic organizer below as you work through the chapter.
   • In the center, write the title of the chapter.
   • When you begin a lesson, write the lesson name in a rectangle.
   • When you complete a lesson, write a skill or key concept in an oval
     linked to that lesson block.
   • When you complete the chapter, use this graphic organizer to help
     you review.

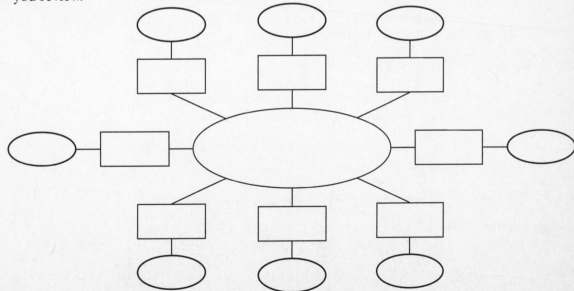

9B: Reading Comprehension

For use after Lesson 9-3

Study Skill: Many reading passages contain a great amount of information. It is essential to recognize which information is necessary for a particular question. You can designate corresponding information by circling, underlining, or boxing that information.

Read the passage below and answer the following questions.

Radioactive material is here today and gone tomorrow. Radioisotopes disintegrate into stable isotopes of different elements at a decreasing rate, but never quite reach zero. Radioactive material is measured in curies (Ci) and 1 Ci = 3.7×10^{10} atoms. A mathematical formula known as the radioactive decay law can measure the rate of radioactive decay and the quantity of material present at any given time. From this formula we obtain a quantity known as half-life. Half-life is known as the period of time required for a quantity of radioactivity to be reduced to one-half its original value. The number following the element symbol is its atomic mass. This is the number of protons and neutrons in its nucleus. The atomic number is just the number of protons. All of this is important when you are studying radioactivity.

Each radioisotope has a unique half-life. For example I-131 has a half-life of 8 days, C-11 has a half-life of 20 minutes, and H-6 has a half-life of 0.8 seconds.

Although this can sound quite difficult, it does not have to be. The following chart can help you calculate the amount of radioactive material that has decayed.

Half-life number	1	2	3	4	5	6	7
Radioactivity remaining	50%	25%	12.5%	6.25%	3.12%	1.56%	0.78%

1. What is the half-life of I-131? _____

2. If you have 100 mCi of I-131, how much would remain after 1 half-life? _____

3. How much would remain after 2 half-lifes? _____

4. How much would remain after 3 half-lifes? _____

5. If 40 mCi was present on January 3rd at noon, how much was remaining on January 19th at noon? _____

6. After 5 half-lifes of a radioactive isotope occur, what percent of the isotope is gone? _____

7. What is the half-life of C-11? _____

8. Suppose your original measure of a sample of C-11 was 25 mCi and now it has only $3\frac{1}{8}$ mCi remaining. How much time has passed? _____

9. You have 50 mCi of H-6, how much remains after 4 seconds? _____

Name_____ Class_____ Date_____

9C: Reading/Writing Math Symbols

For use after Lesson 9-7

Study Skill: Make mental pictures from what you read. This will help you remember it.

In equations and inequalities, *x* and *y* represent coordinates of points, *b* represents the *y*-intercept, and *m* represents the slope. Inequality symbols mean to shade on one side of a boundary line. Match each equation or inequality to the graph that best represents it.

1. $y < b$

2. $x = k$

3. $y = mx + b$; $m > 0$ and $b > 0$

4. $y = b$

5. $y = mx + b$; $m < 0$

6. $y \geq mx + b$

7. $y < mx + b$; $b \neq 0$

8. $y = mx$; $m > 0$

A.
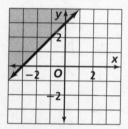

B.
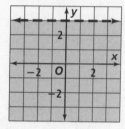

C.
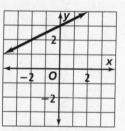

D.
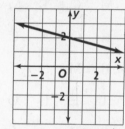

E.
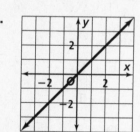

F.
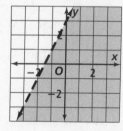

G.
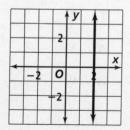

H.
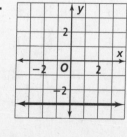

9D: Vocabulary

For use with Chapter Review

Study Skill: When you complete a puzzle such as a word search, remember to read the list of words carefully and completely. As you identify each word in the word search, circle it and then cross off the word from the list. Pay special attention to the spelling of each word.

Complete the word search.

binomial	interest	translation
factor	common ratio	median
monomial	sequence	distributive
standard form	scatter plot	variable
polynomial	outlier	probability
trinomial	reciprocal	degree
systems	elimination	substitution

```
E  Y  R  N  P  O  L  Y  N  O  M  I  A  L  N
L  T  E  E  O  L  A  I  M  O  N  I  R  T  O
I  I  C  J  S  I  S  F  A  C  T  O  R  S  I
M  L  I  L  M  C  T  M  L  Q  H  M  T  E  T
I  I  P  A  R  O  A  U  E  A  P  O  V  Q  A
N  B  R  I  E  M  N  T  T  B  B  Y  U  L
A  A  O  M  I  E  D  O  T  I  S  T  H  E  S
T  B  C  O  L  D  A  L  M  E  T  Y  N  N  N
I  O  A  N  T  I  R  W  Q  I  R  S  S  C  A
O  R  L  I  U  A  D  W  M  U  A  P  B  E  R
N  P  V  B  O  N  F  I  Z  W  W  L  L  U  T
S  Q  C  O  M  M  O  N  R  A  T  I  O  O  S
Q  V  I  N  T  E  R  E  S  T  E  M  S  T  T
E  E  R  G  E  D  M  E  L  B  A  I  R  A  V
E  V  I  T  U  B  I  R  T  S  I  D  G  B  W
```

10A: Graphic Organizer

For use before Lesson 10-1

Study Skill: To help remember formulas and other important information, use a mnemonic. A mnemonic is a memory device to help us associate new information with something familiar. For example, to remember a formula or equation change it into something meaningful. To remember the metric terms kilo, hecto, deka meter, deci, centi, milli, in order, use the first letter of each metric term to represent a word, such as, *k*angaroo *h*ops *d*own *m*ountain *d*rinking *c*hocolate *m*ilk. The key is to create your own then you won't forget them.

Write your answers.

1. What is the chapter title? _____

2. Find the Table of Contents page for this chapter at the front of the book. Name four topics you will study in this chapter.

    _____   _____

    _____   _____

3. What is the topic of the Reading Math page? _____

4. What is the topic of the Test-Taking Strategy page? _____

5. Look through the pages of the chapter. List four real-world connections that you see discussed in this chapter.

    _____   _____

    _____   _____

6. Complete the graphic organizer below as you work through the chapter.
    *   In the center, write the title of the chapter.
    *   When you begin a lesson, write the lesson name in a rectangle.
    *   When you complete a lesson, write a skill or key concept in an oval linked to that lesson block.
    *   When you complete the chapter, use this graphic organizer to help you review.

10B: Reading Comprehension

For use after Lesson 10-4

Study Skill: Many mathematical applications are related to graphs. Many times you are called upon to interpret information given in graphs. Being able to identify the specific parts of a graph will help you to answer questions regarding the graph.

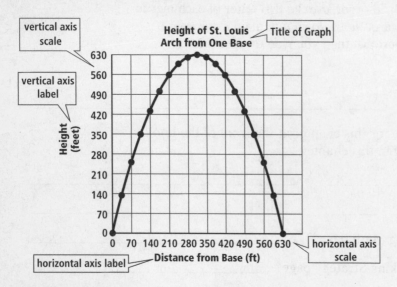

In Exercises 1–7, refer to the graph shown below.

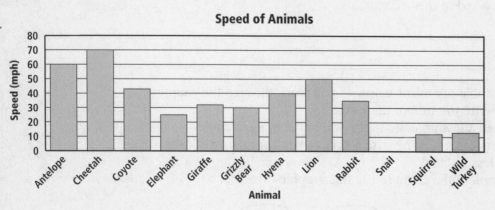

1. What is the title of the graph? _____

2. What is the title of the vertical axis? _____

3. What is the range of the vertical scale? _____

4. What type of graph is this? _____

5. Which two animals have speeds that are the closest to each other?

   _____

6. Which animal is the fastest? _____

7. Which animal is the slowest? _____

10C: Reading/Writing Math Symbols

For use after Lesson 10-8

Study Skill: When interpreting mathematical statements be sure you use the correct words or symbols. Check your written or numerical expressions to make sure you wrote the correct symbols or words.

The graphs below represent the solutions of different linear systems. Some are equations and some are inequalities. The graphs intersect, are parallel, or coincide. Try to match the graphs with the appropriate system, without actually graphing the systems, by looking for symbols and other indicators (such as slopes and *y*-intercepts).

1. $\begin{cases} x + y = 4 \\ 2x - y = 2 \end{cases}$

2. $\begin{cases} 3x - 2y = -2 \\ 3x - 2y = 6 \end{cases}$

3. $\begin{cases} y = 2x - 5 \\ -4x + 2y = -10 \end{cases}$

4. $\begin{cases} x + y \geq 2 \\ x - y \leq 1 \end{cases}$

5. $\begin{cases} 2x - y > 0 \\ x - 2y \leq 1 \end{cases}$

6. $\begin{cases} 2x - 4y \geq 4 \\ x + y < 0 \end{cases}$

A.
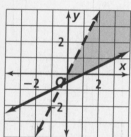

B.
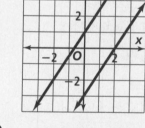

C.
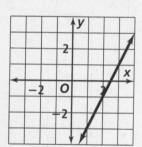

D.
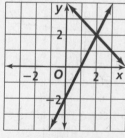

E.
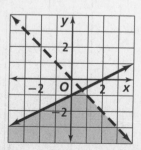

F.
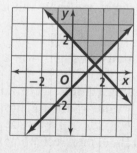

10D: Vocabulary

Study Skill: When taking notes, make your original notes as easy to read as possible. The amount of time needed to interpret messy notes would be better spent rereading and thinking about them.

Fill in the blanks with the word(s) that best completes the sentence.

1. The function $y = ax^2 + bx + c$ is a _____ function.

2. The function $Ax + By = C$ is written in _____ form.

3. The _____ of a monomial is the sum of the exponents of its variables.

4. A _____ is an expression that is a number, a variable, or a product of a number and one or more variables.

5. The fixed number in a geometric sequence is called the _____ ratio.

6. The length of time over which interest is calculated is the _____.

7. When solving a system of linear equations by graphing, any point where all the lines intersect is the _____.

8. A term that has no variable is known as a _____.

9. The "fold" or line that divides a parabola into two matching halves is called the _____.

10. The expression $b^2 - 4ac$ is known as the _____.

11. The _____ of a line is its rate of vertical change over horizontal change.

12. The equation $4(5 - 2 + 3) = 4(5) - 4(2) + 4(3)$ represents the _____ property.

13. A conclusion made by inductive reasoning is called a _____.

14. A relation that assigns exactly one value in the range to each value in the domain is called a _____.

15. Two or more linear equations together form a _____.

16. When a parabola opens upward, the y-coordinate of the vertex is a _____ value of the function.

17. The point at which a parabola intersects the axis of symmetry is called the _____.

11A: Graphic Organizer

For use before Lesson 11-1

Study Skill: After reading a section, recall the information. Ask yourself questions about the section. If you cannot recall enough information reread portions you had trouble remembering. The more time you spend studying the more you can recall.

Write your answers.

1. What is the chapter title? _____

2. Find the Table of Contents page for this chapter at the front of the book. Name four topics you will study in this chapter.

   _____   _____

   _____   _____

3. What is the topic of the Reading Math page? _____

4. What is the topic of the Test-Taking Strategy page? _____

5. Look through the pages of the chapter. List four real-world connections that you see discussed in this chapter.

   _____   _____

   _____   _____

6. Complete the graphic organizer below as you work through the chapter.
   - In the center, write the title of the chapter.
   - When you begin a lesson, write the lesson name in a rectangle.
   - When you complete a lesson, write a skill or key concept in an oval linked to that lesson block.
   - When you complete the chapter, use this graphic organizer to help you review.

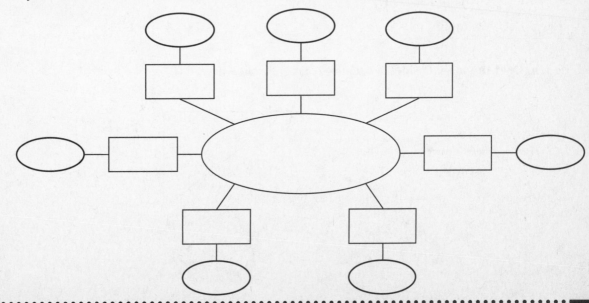

11B: Reading Comprehension

Study Skill: Some math problems have many steps and can be confusing. Sometimes, if you hurry through a problem, you leave out important steps. Think carefully about what the next step to solving a problem might be.

The equations and statements given below are the correct steps and justifications to find the length of b in the right triangle, but they are mixed up. Rearrange the steps and justifications in the correct order.

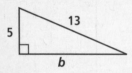

$\sqrt{b^2} = \sqrt{144}$	Simplify.
$25 + b^2 = 169$	Find the principal square root of each side.
$5^2 + b^2 = 13^2$	
$b = 12$	Substitute 5 for a and 13 for c.
$a^2 + b^2 = c^2$	Simplify by squaring each number.
$b^2 = 144$	

Steps	Justifications	Thoughts for organizing steps
$a^2 + b^2 = c^2$		Use the Pythagorean Theorem.
$5^2 + b^2 = 13^2$	Substitute 5 for a and 13 for c.	Replace variables with any known values.
$25 + b^2 = 169$	Simplify by squaring each number.	Perform existing calculations.
$b^2 = 144$	Simplify.	
$\sqrt{b^2} = \sqrt{144}$	Find the principal square root of each side.	More work is needed to isolate the variable.
$b = 12$	Simplify.	

Find the length of the missing side of each right triangle shown.

1.

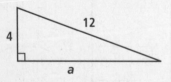

2.

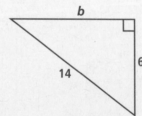

11C: Reading/Writing Math Symbols

For use after Lesson 11-6

Study Skill: When you take notes in any subject, it helps if you learn to use abbreviations and symbols such as @ (at); #, #s (number, numbers); w/ (with); w/o (without); s/b (should be).

Match each written expression or equation in Column A with its symbolic expression or equation in Column B by drawing a line between them.

Column A	Column B
1. eight times x equals 40	**A.** $4x - 2$
2. the square root of xy	**B.** $8x = 40$
3. x divided by y	**C.** $2x^2 - 3y$
4. the square root of the quantity $x + 4$ equals 3	**D.** $5 \leq 8$
5. standard form of a linear equation	**E.** $|x - 3| \leq 4$
6. 5 is less than or equal to 8	**F.** $\sqrt{xy}$
7. feet per mile	**G.** $\sqrt{x + 4} = 3$
8. x squared y to the fourth power	**H.** $3 + x$
9. w divided into 6 equal parts	**I.** $f(x)$
10. eight to the negative two power	**J.** $8 > 5$
11. the quantity x plus four, cubed	**K.** $(x + 4)^3$
12. 2 less than 4 times a number	**L.** $w \div 6$
13. the absolute value of the quantity $x - 3$ less than or equal to 4	**M.** x^2y^4
	N. $(x + 4)^2$
14. kilometers per hour	**O.** $\frac{x}{y}$
15. f of x	**P.** $Ax + By = C$
16. one-third of a number x	**Q.** km/h
17. three plus x	**R.** $\frac{1}{3}x$
18. eight is greater than 5	**S.** 8^{-2}
19. two times x squared minus three times y	**T.** ft/mi
20. the quantity x plus four, squared	

11D: Vocabulary

For use with Chapter Review

Study Skill: When you read, your eyes make small stops along a line of words. Good readers make fewer stops when they read. The more stops you make when you read, the harder it is for you to comprehend what you've read. Try to concentrate and free yourself of distractions as you read.

Complete the crossword puzzle.

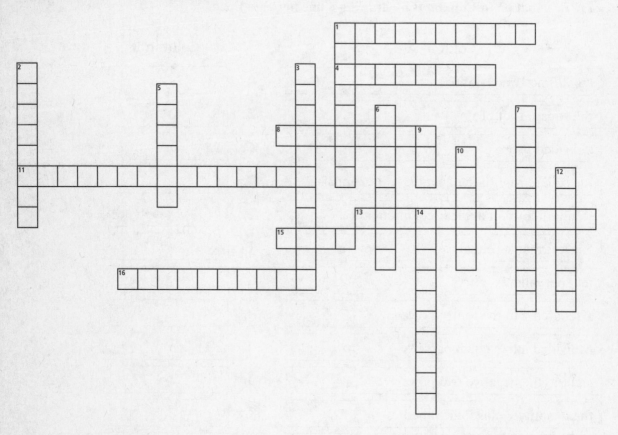

ACROSS	DOWN
1. the sum or difference of two or more monomials	**1.** the graph of a quadratic function
4. the expression under the radical sign	**2.** reversing the *if and then* parts of a statement
8. a polynomial with two terms	**3.** multiplying the numerator and denominator by the same radical expression to simplify the denominator
11. a type of equation with a variable in the radicand	**5.** the highest or lowest point of a parabola
13. the expression under the radical sign in the quadratic formula	**6.** divides a segment into two equal segments
15. opposite side over hypotenuse	**7.** a solution that does not satisfy the original equation
16. side opposite the right angle in a right triangle	**9.** each of the sides forming the right angle of a triangle
	10. adjacent side over hypotenuse
	12. opposite side over adjacent side
	14. the sum and differences of the same two terms

Algebra 1

12A: Graphic Organizer

For use before Lesson 12-1

Study Skill: What do the pages before the first page of Chapter 2 tell you?
Keep notes as you work through each chapter to help you organize your
thinking and to make it easier to review the material when you complete
the chapter.

Write your answers.

1. What is the chapter title? _____

2. Find the Table of Contents page for this chapter at the front of the book.
    Name four topics you will study in this chapter.

    _____   _____

    _____   _____

3. What is the topic of the Reading Math page? _____

4. What is the topic of the Test-Taking Strategy page? _____

5. Look through the pages of the chapter. List four real-world connections
    that you see discussed in this chapter.

    _____   _____

    _____   _____

6. Complete the graphic organizer below as you work through the chapter.
    *   In the center, write the title of the chapter.
    *   When you begin a lesson, write the lesson name in a rectangle.
    *   When you complete a lesson, write a skill or key concept in an oval
        linked to that lesson block.
    *   When you complete the chapter, use this graphic organizer to help
        you review.

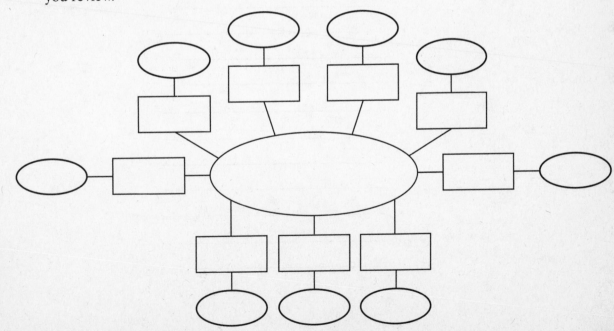

12B: Reading/Writing Math Symbols

For use after Lesson 12-3

Study Skill: It is important to read directions carefully before doing any exercises. Sometimes the directions are asking for more than one answer, or something entirely different than what you think at first glance.

Given the formulas below, write out what the formula means in words, and write a brief description of what the formula is used for or what it represents. The first one is done for you.

1. $a^2 + b^2 = c^2$ leg squared plus leg squared equals hypotenuse squared; Pythagorean Theorem—used to find a side of a right triangle

2. $I = prt$ _____

3. $B = p(1 + r)^x$ _____

4. $a^2 + 2ab + b^2$ _____

5. $ax^2 + bx + c = 0$ _____

6. $b^2 - 4ac$ _____

7. $\tan A = \dfrac{opp}{adj}$ _____

8. $\cos A = \dfrac{adj}{hyp}$ _____

9. $\sin A = \dfrac{opp}{hyp}$ _____

10. $\left(\dfrac{x_1 + x_2}{2}, \dfrac{y_1 + y_2}{2} \right)$ _____

11. $x = \dfrac{-b \pm \sqrt{b^2 - 4ac}}{2a}$ _____

12. $d = \sqrt{(x_2 - x_1)^2 + (y_2 - y_1)^2}$ _____

12C: Reading Comprehension

Study Skill: Some word problems contain so much information it is difficult to know how to deal with it all. Sometimes it helps to organize information in a table.

> Jessica Hernandez bakes and sells gourmet cookies. She bakes two types of cookies: oatmeal and white chocolate macadamia nut. Each batch of oatmeal cookies requires 2 cups of flour and 2 cups of sugar. Each batch of white chocolate macadamia nut cookies requires 3 cups of flour and 1 cup of sugar. Jessica makes a $3 profit on each batch of oatmeal cookies and a $2 profit on each batch of white chocolate macadamia nut cookies. She has 18 cups of flour and 10 cups of sugar on hand. How many batches of each type of cookie should she bake to maximize her profits?

Organize the information you are given into the following table.

	Batches of Cookies	Cups of Flour	Cups of Sugar	Total Profit ($)
Oatmeal	x			
White Chocolate Macadamia Nut	y			
Totals				P

1. What are you asked to find? _____

2. Write an objective function. This is the quantity to be maximized. In this case, that is the total profit. _____

3. Write the constraints as inequalities.

   a. The total number of cups of flour to be used is no more than 18. _____

   b. The total number of cups of sugar to be used is no more than 10. _____

   c. The number of batches of oatmeal cookies to be made is greater than or equal to zero. _____

   d. The total number of batches of white chocolate macadamia nut cookies to be made is greater than or equal to zero. _____

4. Graph the constraints written in Exercise 3.

5. The maximum profit occurs at a vertex of the feasible region. Evaluate the objective function at each vertex. _____

   _____

6. How many batches of each type of cookie need to be made to maximize profit? _____

12D: Vocabulary

For use with Chapter Review

Study Skill: Read aloud or recite the new terms as you read them. This will help you remember and recall rules, definitions and formulas for future use.

Unscramble the UPPERCASE letters to form a math word or phrase that completes each sentence.

1. An METPYSTOA is a line that the graph of a function gets closer and closer to, but does not intersect.

2. A OCMINNOIBAT uses the notation $_nC_r$.

3. An SEVNIER ITVIANARO can be written in the form $xy = k$ or $y = \frac{k}{x}$.

4. A RUTTEAPONMI usess the notation $_nP_r$.

5. A TAIRNLOA OFINUTCN can be written in the form $f(x) = \frac{polynomial}{polynomial}$.

6. The graph of a quadratic function is a BAAPARLO.

7. The quantity $b^2 - 4ac$ is the RIDNMCITSINA of $ax^2 + bx + c = 0$

8. The number b in $y = ab^x$, where $b > 0$, is called the WOHTRG CORFAT.

9. The highest or lowest point on a parabola is its XTERVE.

10. In a right triangle, the NTNATEG ratio compares the length of the side opposite an acute angle to the length of the side adjacent to the same acute angle.

11. You may TAEZIONILRA the denominator of a radical expression when simplifying the expression.

12. The DIDRAANC is the expression under the radical sign.

Answers

Chapter 1A

1. Tools of Algebra   **2.** Answers may vary. Sample: order of operations, adding real numbers, subtracting real numbers, and the Distributive Property   **3.** Reading an Example
4. Writing Gridded Responses   **5.** Answers may vary. Sample: sales, sports, shopping, cars   **6.** Check students' work. Chapter: Tools of Algebra; Using Variables: model relationships; Exponents and Order of Operations: simplifying and evaluating expressions; Exploring Real Numbers: classifying numbers; Adding Real Numbers: adding real numbers; Subtracting Real Numbers: subtracting real numbers; Multiplying and Dividing Real Numbers: multiplying and dividing; The Distributive Property: simplifying algebraic expressions with the Distributive Property; Properties of Real Numbers: identifying properties; Graphing Data on the Coordinate Plane: graphing points on the coordinate plane

Chapter 1B

1. 3 multiplied by 7 *or* 3 times 7   **2.** 5 multiplied by the variable n or 5 times n **3.** 3 divided by 4   **4.** 7 divided by 12
5. Use 2 as a factor x times or 2 to the x power
6. 6 multiplied by 7 or 6 times 7   **7.** $7 - 3$ **8.** $p \div 2$ or $\frac{p}{2}$
9. $4 \div x$ or $\frac{4}{x}$ **10.** $y = 9$

Chapter 1C

1. the blue whale   **2.** the weight of the whale   **3.** About how much of the total weight of the whale was *not* the skeleton?
4. 50,000 pounds   **5.** pounds   **6.** 160 tons   **7.** tons
8. Multiply 160 tons by 2000 lb/ton.   **9.** 320,000 lb – 50,000 lb $= w$ so $w = 270{,}000$ lb   **10.** About 270,000 pounds of the total weight are *not* skeleton.

Chapter 1D

1. real   **2.** constant   **3.** base   **4.** like   **5.** open   **6.** power
7. natural   **8.** origin   **9.** term   **10.** element

Chapter 2A

1. Solving Equations   **2.** Answers may vary. Sample: solving one-step equations, solving multi-step equations, equations and problem solving, and formulas   **3.** Reading for Problem Solving   **4.** Writing Short Responses   **5.** Answers may vary. Sample: catalog purchasing, construction, recreation, travel
6. Check students' work.   Chapter: Solving Equations; Solving One-Step Equations: solving equations using addition, subtraction, multiplication, or division; Solving Two-Step Equations: solving equations using two steps; Solving Multi-Step Equations: using the distributive property to solve equations; Equations With Variables on Both Sides: solving equations with variables on both sides; Equations and Problem Solving: defining a variable in terms of another variable; Formulas: transforming literal equations; Using Measures of Central Tendency: finding mean, median, and mode

Chapter 2B

1. M   **2.** L   **3.** G   **4.** C   **5.** H   **6.** B   **7.** E   **8.** N   **9.** J   **10.** O
11. I   **12.** D   **13.** F   **14.** A   **15.** K

Chapter 2C

the distance between the colleges
They both planned to leave at 8:00.
Robin has a heavy foot.
returning to college after break

Chapter 2D

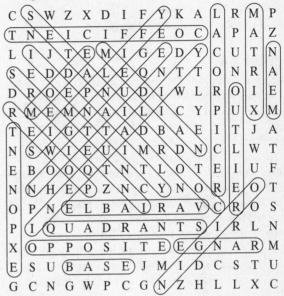

Chapter 3A

1. Solving Inequalities   **2.** Answers may vary. Sample: inequalities and their graphs, solving inequalities using addition and subtraction, solving multi-step inequalities, and compound inequalities   **3.** Reading to Analyze Errors
4. Writing Extended Responses   **5.** Answers may vary. Sample: air travel, safe loads, community service, chemistry
6. Check students' work. Chapter: Solving Inequalities; Inequalities and their Graphs: identifying solutions to inequalities; Solving Inequalities using Addition and Subtraction: using addition and subtraction to solve inequalities; Solving Inequalities Using Multiplication and Division: using multiplication and division to solve inequalities; Solving Multi-Step Inequalities: solving multi-step inequalities with variables on one or two sides; Compound Inequalities: Solving and graphing compound inequalities; Absolute Value Equations and Inequalities: solving equations that involve absolute value

Chapter 3B

1. is less than   **2.** is greater than   **3.** is less than or equal to
4. is greater than or equal to   **5.** is equal to   **6.** 8 is greater than 4.
7. 12 is less than 25.   **8.** $3x$ is less than or equal to 15.
9. $4x$ plus 2 is greater than or equal to 12.
10. $12x$ equals 36.   **11.** $8 < 12$ **12.** $17 > 2$ **13.** $12x > 36$.
14. $15x - 8 < 32$ **15.** $8(4x - 3) = 21$ **16.** $10x + 4 \geq 15$
17. $3x - 12 \leq 21$ **18.** $32x = 12 + 4x$

Chapter 3C

1. C **2.** H **3.** J **4.** A **5.** J **6.** A **7.** L **8.** E **9.** D
10. B **11.** F **12.** K

Chapter 3D

1. compound inequalities **2.** identity **3.** range **4.** outlier
5. exponent **6.** quadrants **7.** simplify **8.** variable
9. coefficient **10.** whole numbers **11.** reciprocal
12. Mathematics is the queen of the sciences

Chapter 4A

1. Solving and Applying Proportions **2.** Answers may vary.
Sample: ratio and proportion, proportions and percent
equations, percent of change, and probability of compound
events **3.** Reading a Formula **4.** Making Quantitative
Comparisons **5.** Answers may vary. Sample: bicycle racing,
map distances, agriculture, animal population **6.** Check
students' work. Chapter: Solving and Applying Proportions;
Ratio and Proportions: solving proportions; Proportions and
Similar Figures: using similar figures when measuring
indirectly; Proportions and Percent Equations: writing and
solving percent equations; Percent of Change: finding percent
of change and percent error; Applying Ratios to Probability:
finding theoretical and experimental probability; Probability
of Compound Events: finding the probability of independent
and dependent events

Chapter 4B

1. cents per ounce **2.** miles per hour **3.** feet per minute
4. kilometers per hour **5.** feet per mile **6.** dollars per year
7. dollars per pound **8.** feet per week **9.** gallons per week
10. miles per gallon **11.** pounds per square inch
12. feet per second squared **13.** meters per second squared

14. dollars per ounce **15.** mi/gal **16.** $/lb **17.** km/h
18. ft/min

Chapter 4C

1. correct **2.** $10 = 0.05x$ **3.** correct **4.** correct
5. $0.275(152) = x$ **6.** $\frac{24}{48} = x$ or $48x = 24$ **7.** $\frac{132}{82.5} = x$ or
$82.5x = 132$ **8.** correct **9.** correct **10.** correct
11. $90(0.75) = x$ **12.** $\frac{25}{300} = x$ **13.** $(0.20)(18) = x$
14. $80,000(0.06) = x$

Chapter 4D

1. L **2.** J **3.** F **4.** M **5.** H **6.** C **7.** G **8.** A **9.** E **10.** I
11. O **12.** D **13.** N **14.** B **15.** K

Chapter 5A

1. Graphs and Functions **2.** Answers may vary. Sample:
relating graphs to events, relations and functions, writing a
function rule, and direct variation **3.** Reading a Graph
4. Using a Variable **5.** Answers may vary. Sample: cooking,
business, water conservation, weather **6.** Check students' work.

Chapter 5B

1. H **2.** I **3.** S **4.** C **5.** O **6.** G **7.** K **8.** D **9.** J
10. E **11.** F **12.** M **13.** Q **14.** B **15.** A **16.** L **17.** T
18. P **19.** N **20.** R

Chapter 5C

1. about 450 cm^3 **2.** about 26 servings

Chapter 5D

Algebra 1: Reading and Math Literacy Masters Answers (continued)

Chapter 6A

1. Linear Equations and Their Graphs **2.** Answers may vary. Sample: rate of change and slope, slope-intercept form, standard form, scatter plots and equations of lines **3.** Reading Math Vocabulary **4.** Drawing a Diagram **5.** Answers may vary. Sample: plant growth, commission, health and fitness, urban planning **6.** Check students' work.

Chapter 6B

1. function: slope = 2, y-intercept = 3
2. relation
3. function: slope = -4, y-intercept = -3
4. function: slope = $\frac{3}{4}$, y-intercept = 2
5. relation
6. function: slope = $-\frac{2}{3}$, y-intercept = -1

Chapter 6C

1. x-intercept **2.** is greater than **3.** absolute value of x **4.** is perpendicular to **5.** is greater than or equal to **6.** slope-intercept form of an equation **7.** is less than **8.** standard form of an equation **9.** is equal to **10.** is parallel to **11.** slope **12.** y-intercept **13.** is less than or equal to **14.** the opposite of x **15.** y-intercept **16.** multiply

Chapter 6D

1. Parallel lines **2.** y-intercept **3.** slope-intercept **4.** slope **5.** perpendicular **6.** translation **7.** range **8.** function rule **9.** Independent **10.** median **11.** base **12.** variable **13.** reciprocal **14.** Commutative Property of Addition **15.** decrease **16.** complement of an event **17.** absolute value **18.** sequence

Chapter 7A

1. Systems of Equations and Inequalities **2.** Answers may vary. Sample: solving systems by graphing, solving systems using substitution, linear inequalities, systems of linear inequalities **3.** Reading for Problem Solving **4.** Finding Multiple Correct Answers **5.** Answers may vary. Sample: communication, transportation, agriculture, sports **6.** Check students' work.

Chapter 7B

1. C **2.** A **3.** D **4.** B

Chapter 7C

1. $y = 1, y = 5, x = 1, x = 5$ **2.** -2

Chapter 7D

1. B **2.** I **3.** O **4.** D **5.** M **6.** F **7.** J **8.** N **9.** A **10.** R **11.** G **12.** P **13.** K **14.** C **15.** H **16.** Q **17.** E **18.** L

Chapter 8A

1. Exponents and Exponential Functions **2.** Answers may vary. Sample: zero and negative exponents, scientific notation, properties of exponents, exponential functions **3.** Reading a Graph **4.** Testing Multiple Choices **5.** Answers may vary. Sample: population growth, astronomy, medicine, recycling **6.** Check students' work.

Chapter 8B

1. 2 times x cubed, y to the fourth power **2.** 4 to the negative third power **3.** x squared **4.** the quantity x times y **5.** the quantity x squared, cubed **6.** the quantity y cubed, z to the fourth power, squared **7.** x divided by y **8.** the quantity y squared divided by x to the fourth power, to the fifth power **9.** 5 times x times y to the fourth power **10.** x to the fifth power plus x to the fifth power **11.** the square root of the quantity x squared y **12.** 8 times x squared minus 3 times y **13.** 8 times y cubed divided by the quantity 3 times x to the eighth power **14.** x squared divided by x to the eighth power **15.** 4 times x to the eleventh power

Chapter 8C

1. 80 ft **2.** 10 m **3.** 645 cm or 6.45 m

Chapter 8D

1. scientific notation **2.** term **3.** geometric **4.** substitution **5.** no solution **6.** increase **7.** compound **8.** interest **9.** domain **10.** power **11.** perpendicular **12.** mode **13.** outcome **14.** element **15.** growth **16.** real numbers

Chapter 9A

1. Polynomials and Factoring **2.** Answers may vary. Sample: adding and subtracting polynomials, multiplying special cases, factoring special cases, factoring by grouping **3.** Reading a Diagram **4.** Eliminating Answers **5.** Answers may vary. Sample: manufacturing, genetics, sales, construction **6.** Check students' work.

Chapter 9B

1. 8 days **2.** 50 mCi **3.** 25 mCi **4.** 12.5 mCi **5.** 10 mCi **6.** 96.88% **7.** 20 minutes **8.** 1 hour **9.** 3.125 mCi

Chapter 9C

1. B **2.** G **3.** C **4.** H **5.** D **6.** A **7.** F **8.** E

Chapter 9D

```
E Y R N P O L Y N O M I A L N
L T E O L A I M O N I R T O
I I C J S I S F A C T O R S I
M L I L M C T M L Q H M T E T
I I P A R O A U E A P O V Q A
N B R A M N T T T B B Y U L
A O O M E I D O T I S T H E S
T R C L T D A L M E T Y N N E
I P A I U I R W Q I R S S C Q
O R L B O A N D W M U A P B E U
N P V B O N F I Z W W L L U T E
S Q C O M M O N R A T I O S N
Q V I N T E R E S T E M S T C
E E R G E D M E L B A I R A V
E V I T U B I R T S I D G B W
```

Chapter 10A

1. Quadratic Equations and Functions 2. Answers may vary. Sample: quadratic functions, solving quadratic equations, completing the square, using the discriminant
3. Using a Formula 4. Choosing "Cannot be Determined"
5. Answers may vary. Sample: gravity, fireworks, construction, city planning 6. Check students' work.

Chapter 10B

1. speed of animals 2. speed (mph) 3. 0 to 80 4. bar graph
5. squirrel and wild turkey 6. cheetah 7. snail

Chapter 10C

1. D 2. B 3. C 4. F 5. A 6. E

Chapter 10D

1. quadratic 2. standard 3. degree 4. monomial
5. common 6. interest period 7. solution 8. constant
9. axis of symmetry 10. discriminant 11. slope
12. distributive 13. conjecture 14. function
15. system 16. minimum 17. vertex

Chapter 11A

1. Radical Expressions and Equations 2. Answers may vary. Sample: simplifying radicals, the distance and midpoint formulas, solving radical equations, trigonometric ratios
3. Reading for Problem Solving 4. Using Estimation
5. Answers may vary. Sample: tourism, fire rescue, archaeology, investments, packaging, navigation
6. Check students' work.

Chapter 11B

1. 11.3 2. 12.6

Chapter 11C

1. B 2. F 3. O 4. G 5. P 6. D 7. T 8. M 9. L 10. S
11. K 12. A 13. E 14. Q 15. I 16. R 17. H 18. J
19. C 20. N

Chapter 11D

Algebra 1: Reading and Math Literacy Masters Answers (continued)

Chapter 12A

1. Rational Expressions and Functions **2.** Answers may vary. Sample: inverse variations, simplifying rational expressions, dividing polynomials, counting methods and permutations **3.** Reading an Example **4.** Answering the Question Asked **5.** Answers may vary. Sample: surveying, air travel, encryption, jury selection **6.** Check students' work.

Chapter 12B

1. leg squared plus leg squared equals hypotenuse squared; Pythagorean Theorem—used to find a side of a right triangle **2.** Interest equals principal times rate times time; calculate interest **3.** Base equals principal times the quantity 1 plus the rate to the x power; compound interest formula **4.** a squared plus 2 times a times b plus b squared; a perfect square trinomial **5.** a times x squared plus b times x plus c equals zero; standard form of a quadratic equation **6.** b squared minus 4 times a times c; discriminant—find the number of roots of a quadratic formula **7.** tangent of an angle equals the opposite side divided by the adjacent side; tangent formula—used to determine a leg or angle in a right triangle **8.** cosine of an angle equals the adjacent side divided by the hypotenuse; cosine formula—used to determine a side or angle in a right triangle **9.** sine of an angle equals the opposite side divided by the hypotenuse; sine formula—used to determine a side or angle in a right triangle **10.** the sum of the x-coordinates of two points divided by 2, and sum of the y-coordinates of two points divided by 2; Midpoint Formula—find the midpoint of a segment **11.** x equals the opposite of b plus or minus the square root of b squared minus 4 times a times c, divided by 2 times a; Quadratic Formula—solve quadratic equations **12.** the distance equals the square root of the difference of the x-coordinates, squared, plus the difference of the y-coordinates, squared; Distance Formula—find the length of a segment or the distance between two points

Chapter 12C

	Batches of Cookies	Cups of Flour	Cups of Sugar	Total Profit ($)
Oatmeal	x	$2x$	$2x$	$3x$
White Chocolate Macadamia Nut	y	$3y$	y	$2y$
Totals		18	10	P

1. You are asked to find the number of batches of each type of cookie Jessica should make to maximize profit. **2.** $P = 3x + 2y$ **3a.** $2x + 3y \leq 18$ **3b.** $2x + y \leq 10$ **3c.** $x \geq 0$ **3d.** $y \geq 0$

4.

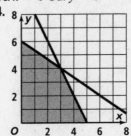

5. Vertex: $(0, 0)$, $P = \$0$; Vertex: $(5, 0)$, $P = \$15$; Vertex: $(0, 6)$, $P = \$12$; Vertex: $(3, 4)$, $P = \$17$ **6.** To maximize profits Jessica would need to make 3 batches of oatmeal and 4 batches of white chocolate macadamia nut cookies.

Chapter 12D

1. asymptote **2.** combination **3.** inverse variation **4.** permutation **5.** rational function **6.** parabola **7.** discriminant **8.** growth factor **9.** vertex **10.** tangent **11.** rationalize **12.** radicand